REALLY, REALLY BIG QUESTIONS

about God, Faith, and Religion

KINGFISHER
LONDON & NEW YORK

Published in the United States by Kingfisher,
175 Fifth Ave., New York, NY 10010
Kingfisher is an imprint of Macmillan Children's Books, London.

Distributed in the U.S. and Canada by Macmillan,
175 Fifth Ave., New York, NY 10010

Library of Congress Cataloging-in-Publication data has been applied for.

ISBN: 978-0-7534-6678-0

Kingfisher books are available for special promotions and premiums.
For details contact: Special Markets Department, Macmillan,
175 Fifth Ave., New York, NY 10010.

For more information, please visit www.kingfisherbooks.com

Printed in China
1 3 5 7 9 8 6 4 2
1TR/0511/WKT/UNTD/140WF

REALLY, REALLY BIG QUESTIONS

about God, Faith, and Religion

Dr. Julian Baggini

Illustrated by

Nishant Choksi

CONTENTS

CHAPTER 1
A RAINBOW OF RELIGIONS

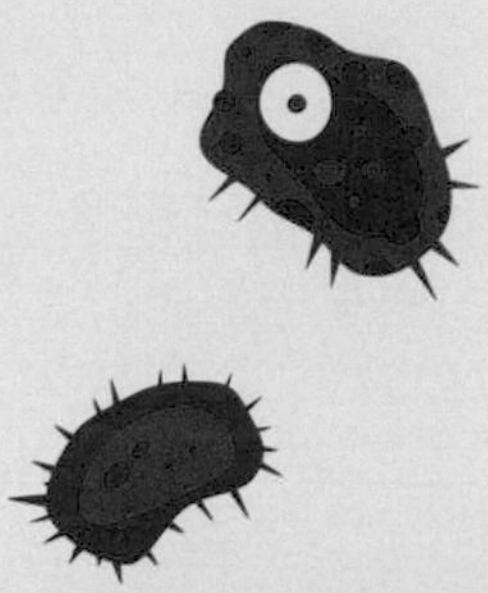

CHAPTER 2
SEARCHING FOR GOD

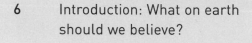

CHAPTER 3
SAINTS, SINNERS, GOOD, AND EVIL

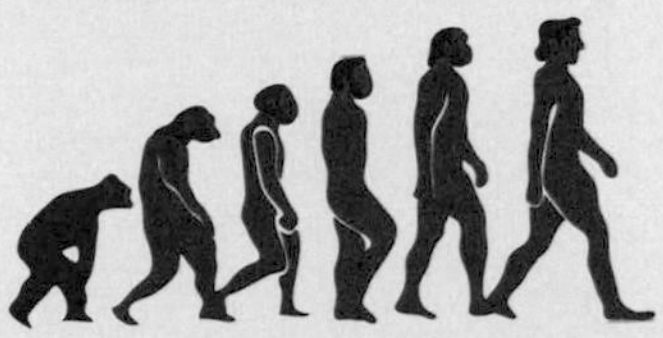

CHAPTER 4
LIVING WITH FAITH, GOD, SOULS, AND ANGELS

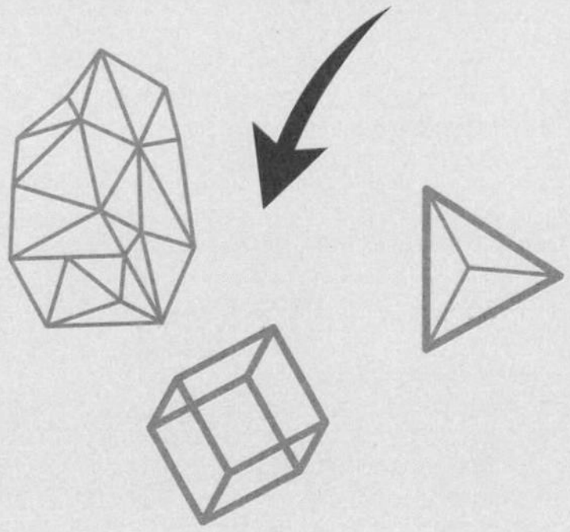

INTRODUCTION

WHAT ON EARTH SHOULD WE BELIEVE?

DR. JULIAN BAGGINI

Imagine you are a visitor to Earth from outer space. You would find a world of astonishing variety. From the window of your flying saucer, you would see vast seas of ice and snow, enormous mountain ranges, fields, forests, and huge, flat deserts. You would see people living in tiny villages and in cities of millions.

But almost everywhere you went in the world, you would find signs of the same thing: *religion*. You would see a religious building—a church, a mosque, a synagogue, a temple—in almost every village, town, or city. You would see people praying to or worshiping their gods, some regularly, some only from time to time. You would see religious symbols, such as crosses, in people's houses or worn around their necks.

"Religion is clearly very important to these earthlings," you might think.

But what is this thing called "religion"? Although it is everywhere, *why is it so different in different places?* Why do so many people believe it, and why do some reject it? What does each religion mean to its followers? Would the world be the same *without* religion?

Until you had answered questions like these, you wouldn't really understand earthlings and how they live. And that's also true if you are an earthling yourself, which I very much hope you are! To understand the world we live in, we need to understand the religions that fill it. And to do that, we're going to have to ask some really, really big questions . . .

1

A RAINBOW OF RELIGIONS

All over the world, throughout history, we find religions. Each one is different. For example, in Christianity, Islam, and Judaism, there is only one God, but in Hinduism, there seem to be many. In Buddhism, there are no gods at all.

Why is there so much variety? Which religion, if any, should we believe? And how should we deal with the fact that people disagree about the really important things religions tell us?

WHAT IS RELIGION?

Religions have three things in common.

First, they involve a set of beliefs about how the world was created, why we are here, and how we should live. In almost every religion, some of these beliefs are *supernatural*. This doesn't mean that religious people believe in ghosts or witches. All it means is that religious people believe there is more to our world than what we see around us in nature. There is also God, gods, souls, or spirits.

Second, religions almost always involve certain *activities*. Believers do things like pray, worship, meditate, read holy books, and give money to the poor. Religion is not only about what you *think*—it's also about what you *do*.

Third, religions are usually communities of some kind. To belong to a religion is to belong to a group of people who meet together and help one another.

HOW DO WE UNDERSTAND RELIGION?

People who have different beliefs from our own can seem weird! A Christian, for example, might think it's funny that one of the Hindu gods, Ganesh, has the head of an elephant. But a Hindu might find it even more bizarre that a common Christian ceremony, Communion, apparently involves eating the body and blood of Jesus.

Accepting that our beliefs can appear just as strange as other people's may help us realize that *we are not that different after all*.

So how do we *understand* religion? We can look at what different religions' special books tell us. We can read the Bible to understand Christianity, the Koran to understand Islam, or the Bhagavad-Gita to understand Hinduism.

We can also listen to what *religious leaders* say. Rabbis teach their communities about Judaism, while imams are Muslim leaders. The Pope is an authority on what Roman Catholicism means today, while the Dalai Lama speaks for Tibetan Buddhism.

Books and leaders do not tell us *everything*, however. People disagree about the meaning of the stories in religious books, and religious leaders can disagree among themselves.

So we can't just ask people for the answers to the really big questions we have about religion, and we can't just look them up—even in this book! *We have to think for ourselves*.

WHY ARE THERE SO MANY RELIGIONS?

There are *so many different religions* in the world that counting them isn't easy. Even if you stick to the biggest ones, there are more than 20 with more than half a million followers each.

So why is there all this variety?

One possibility is that only one, or some, of the world's religions are true and that the rest are mistakes. One problem with that answer is, *how do we know which one is right?*

Another possibility is that every religion is wrong in some way, but many—perhaps all—have gotten *some* things right.

A third possibility is that religions are all just *human inventions*. Of course, people don't think they are just making it up. Religious people genuinely believe they have discovered truths and not just invented stories. But maybe they are wrong.

Which is the right answer? I can't tell you that. You have to decide for yourself which one makes the most sense.

"But, Marge, what if we chose the wrong religion? Each week we just make God madder and madder."

Homer Simpson
From cartoon series *The Simpsons*

WHY ARE THERE DIFFERENT KINDS OF THE SAME RELIGION?

There are so many different religions that if you were to buy them from a store, it would have to be a huge supermarket. And just as supermarkets sell different varieties of the same thing—pasta, candy bars, laundry detergents—many of the world's religions offer different varieties, too.

For example, among the world's two billion Christians, you'll find Roman Catholics, Anglicans, Methodists, Eastern Orthodox Christians, Baptists, Presbyterians . . . the list could go on and on.

The reason for this is that over time, *a religion often splits into different groups*. These groups may then undergo their own divisions, and so on. You can see how easily religions multiply!

But *why* does a religion split in the first place? Usually it's because its members disagree—either about what the teachings of the religion should be or about who has the right to hold power within it.

Because religious people are human, they get caught up in the same kinds of rivalries and power games that other human beings do, too.

So, in a way, there's no mystery about why religions split: *religious people disagree because all people disagree, religious or not!*

SHOULD WE RESPECT PEOPLE FROM DIFFERENT RELIGIONS?

In some parts of the world, at some times in history, people were expected to follow one religion and *one religion only*. Those who refused were either thrown out of their country, imprisoned, or killed.

Nowadays, the United Nations recognizes the freedom to practice the religion of our choice as a basic human right.

We respect people with different beliefs because we know that religion matters very much to people, and even if we think they are wrong, we cannot be sure that we are right. Respect involves accepting that *no one knows for sure what the truth about God and religion is*.

However, that does not mean that we must respect *anything* that people do, even if they say they do it because of their religion. We do not respect people who kill others in the name of their religion or who persecute those who disagree with them. We respect people's right to believe as long as they behave in a good and decent way. That sounds fair, doesn't it?

WHY ARE SOME COUNTRIES MORE RELIGIOUS THAN OTHERS?

A few years ago, a survey discovered that nine out of ten people in Africa said they were religious. In Latin America and the Middle East, eight out of ten people said they were. But in western Europe, only six out of ten people said they were religious.

So why are some parts of the world more religious than others? Well, it often seems that richer countries with more education are less religious.

But it is not as simple as that. The United States is a very religious country, with more than seven out of every ten people describing themselves as religious. But it is also the richest country in the world, with high levels of education. All over the world, there are people who are rich, educated, *and* religious.

So although wealth and education do play a role, we must look at the *history and culture of each individual country* to see why people there believe what they do. There are so many factors involved that it's hard to figure out why some countries are more religious than others!

CAN WE CRITICIZE RELIGION?

Some people get very angry when other people criticize their religion. And some people have even been killed because they criticized another person's religion.

But criticism can be a *good thing*—although it depends on what you *mean* by criticism. It doesn't just mean to say bad things about something; criticism also means to debate, to analyze, to discuss something fully and give your opinion. Unless you think that all religions are perfect, you must think that this sort of criticism should be allowed.

So remember, what's important is *how* you criticize. The best criticism is not rude, but polite and helpful—the way your teacher might comment on your homework or a sports coach might assess his or her players.

But make sure you know your facts first—*you can't discuss someone else's religion if you don't know enough about it!*

WAS THERE REALLY A GREAT FLOOD?

The Christian Bible, the Jewish Torah, and the Muslim Koran all contain remarkable stories of miracles and strange events.

One of the most famous is the Great Flood. In the version shared by Jews and Christians, God says to a good man named Noah:

"I am going to bring floodwaters on the earth to destroy all life under the heavens, every creature that has the breath of life in it."

He tells Noah to build a big boat, an ark, to save his family and "two of all living creatures, male and female." The floods come, and the ark saves Noah, his family, and all the animals. Life on Earth continues.

But could this *really* have happened?

How could Noah have found room for two of *every single type of animal,* even in a huge boat? How could there ever have been enough rain to flood *the entire world?* And how would he have gotten ahold of *penguins* in his Middle Eastern home? Perhaps you can think of other reasons why the flood might seem unlikely.

Most people don't think the Great Flood really happened. The same is true of other incredible stories, like the one about Jonah, who was swallowed by a whale and lived to tell the tale. Most people think they are *stories*, not *historical facts*. But such stories can be important, too. They can teach believers about what God wants and how we should live.

Some people, however, do believe that all the stories in their holy books really did happen. What do *you* think?

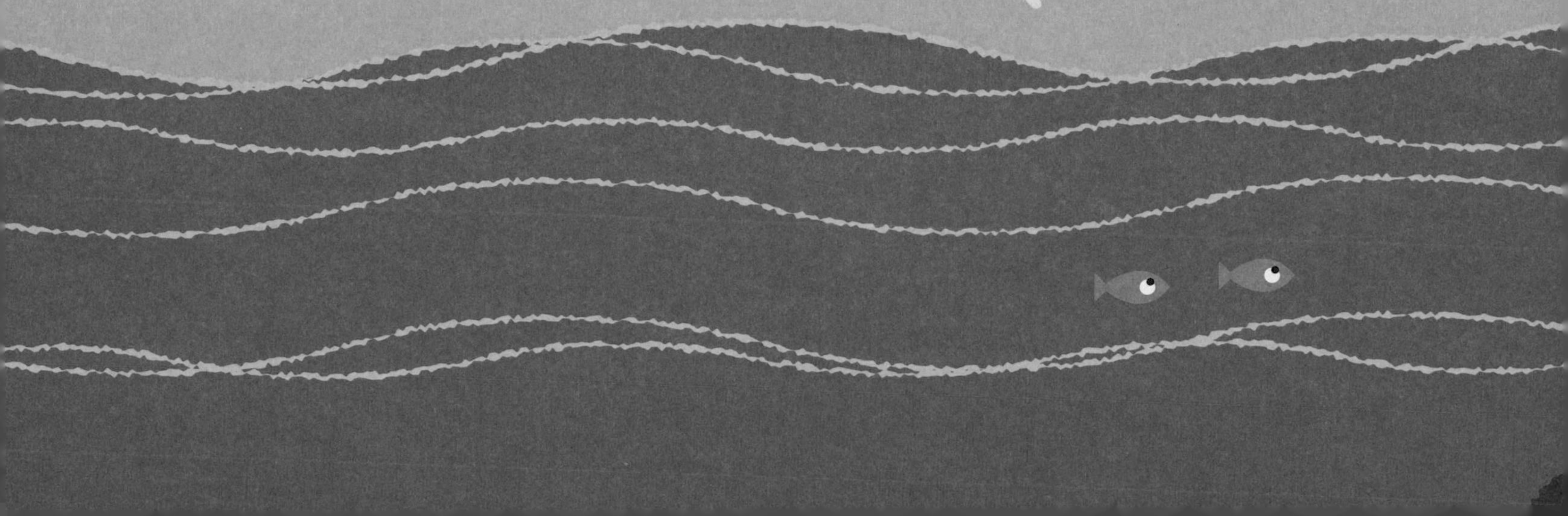

2

SEARCHING FOR GOD

Who's in charge around here? I don't mean of your house, your school, or your town—I mean of *the world, the universe, the whole thing!* Maybe *nobody* is (and maybe that's why it rains when you're on vacation and too much chocolate makes your teeth fall out).

But many religions say that the universe does have *some kind of controller*. And for most people, that controller is an amazing being called God. *God* made us, *God* takes care of us, *God* will reward us if we do the right thing and punish us if we do wrong. And God can do *anything*. Sounds pretty amazing, eh? So where is this God?

Let's go take a look for him.

Or is it a *her?*
Or an *it?*
Or even a *them?*

WHAT IS GOD?

Those who believe in God all agree that, whatever he is, he's far more amazing than any human being. Most people think he has *three superpowers*.

First, he's *all-knowing*. You can't hide anything from him. Planning a surprise party for him would be a complete waste of time.

Second, he's *all-powerful*. He can do *anything*. Most religious people believe he created the entire universe.

Third, he is *all-loving*. Some people think he is willing to punish the wicked, but all he really wants is the best for us, his creations.

All-knowing, all-powerful, and all-loving—sounds like he's got it all!

"If God did not exist,
it would be necessary
to invent him."

Voltaire (1694–1778)
French philosopher

DOES GOD EXIST?

God may sound incredible, but remember *incredible* literally means "unbelievable." So is the idea of God hard to believe? Could such an amazing being really exist?

Nonreligious people who don't believe that God exists are known as *atheists*. There are also some people, such as Buddhists, who are religious but do not believe in God. And there are many *animist religions*, whose followers believe not in God but in spirits that are part of all living things.

Even when two people both say they *do* believe in God, it sometimes turns out that they have very different ideas about *who God is*. So even when people agree that God does exist, they might disagree about *which* God exists!

COULD THERE BE MORE THAN ONE GOD?

Some religions have gods, but not the single, superpowerful God most people are familiar with from Christianity, Judaism, and Islam. Instead, they believe in *many gods*, ones that take care of different parts of the world or of life. In ancient Greek religion, for example, Aphrodite was the goddess of love and beauty and Poseidon was the god of the sea.

Many people know that Hinduism is a religion with thousands of gods. Some see these gods as forms in which the one true God, Brahman, shows himself to us. Some believe that Brahman is like a person who thinks about us and cares for us, whereas others believe that Brahman is more like a supreme force or energy.

Nowadays, the world's biggest religions believe in one God and one God only. But the most popular view is not always the right one. Maybe there are many gods; maybe there are none.

GOD?
BIG BANG!
{ Vn (w) }
H_2O
Vn^2 E (-) (HC₂ = 1)
H2 = 1(V₂)
(V = Nv)
{23 0001 01}
V = 2.00001
{ V + Nv(c) (-) }
24/12
$E = MC^2$
{1} M(Vs)
{11} 2 x = (v)

CAN WE PROVE GOD EXISTS?

We can't scientifically observe God, like we can animals, objects, or places, but nonetheless some people think they can prove he exists. That would be pretty impressive! However, most people think these "proofs" don't work.

One such argument is that *everything must have a cause*. Even the cause of the universe—the big bang—itself had a cause. But you can't keep going back to earlier causes forever. Eventually, you have to end up with *a first cause*—something that was powerful and amazing enough to create the big bang and the universe but that wasn't created by anything else. What could be that amazing? *God,* of course!

The problem is that if you state that *everything must have a cause,* you can't avoid the question, "What caused God?" But if you say that *nothing caused God,* then it's not true that everything must have a cause! So maybe the universe doesn't need a cause and the existence of God is not necessary after all.

Another argument is that the universe is so wonderfully well organized that *something must have designed it*. Think of the way the bees, the plants, the sun, and the rain all fit so well together, so that life keeps growing throughout the seasons.

The trouble is that science has helped explain—without the need for a god—how it is that different life forms depend on one another. It may look as though it's all beautifully "designed," but maybe there's no design at all—it's just *nature* taking its course.

There are other arguments, and people spend whole lifetimes arguing for or against them. But most serious thinkers about religion do not think that God's existence can be proved. There may be good reasons for or against believing in God, but there is no single proof that can settle the issue once and for all. That's why we're still disagreeing about it after many thousands of years of human existence!

WHAT DOES GOD LOOK LIKE?

Vatican City in Rome, Italy, is the home of the Roman Catholic Church, the world's biggest Christian group. If you go to the palace of the Pope, the church's leader, and into the Sistine Chapel, look up at the ceiling. You'll see one of the most famous paintings of God ever.

He is shown as an old but strong man, with white hair and a beard. He reaches out his finger to give life to Adam, the first human being.

When Christianity's God is pictured, it is usually something like this. Presenting him that way makes him seem wise, mature, kind, and approachable.

It helps us have an idea of God, but Michelangelo's painting on the ceiling of the chapel does not show us what he *really* looks like. What God really looks like is a *mystery*.

Some religious traditions, such as those of Judaism and Islam, do not allow their followers to make any images of God at all. God's appearance is completely unknown, they say, and it is sinful even to attempt to guess what it is.

Whether religions allow us to picture God or not, no one can really say what God looks like.

IS GOD A MAN?

Look at all those pictures of the Christian God and what you almost always see is an old *man*. Read religious texts and God is "He" and often called "Our Father." So does that mean God is definitely a man?

If that's what the holy books say, some people believe, then it must be true.

But there's something odd about that. You find males and females among animals and people because animals and people produce children. But God is not an animal—or even a person like you or me. And although Jesus is said to be the son of God, he is not God's child in a "normal" father-and-son way.

So why is God usually thought of as being a man? *Do we need to think of God as having a gender at all?*

Although God is beyond our complete understanding, perhaps we have to talk about him (and paint him) in ways that fit what we think we do understand about him. We think of God as a man because that helps us imagine him better.

But why a *man?* Why not a *woman*?

The answer is probably that for most of human history, men have had more power than women. Our image of the most powerful being in the universe was created in the image of the most powerful people on Earth—men.

DID GOD CREATE THE WORLD?

Most people who believe in God think that he did one very important thing: he created the universe, including our world and everything in it. Almost every religion has a story about how he did this. One Hindu story has the God of creation, Brahma, making the world from the leaves of a lotus flower. In the Christian and Jewish traditions, God created the heavens and Earth over six days and rested on the seventh day.

Some people think these stories are completely true. Most, however, think they are just colorful ways of expressing the idea that God created the world in some way, perhaps in a way that we don't understand.

All these stories, however, came before modern science. We now know that the universe began almost 14 billion years ago with the big bang. Our Sun and our planet, Earth, began to take shape just over four and a half billion years ago, and human beings evolved about 200,000 years ago. Almost every scientist agrees that we do not need God to explain any of these developments.

CAN GOD DO ANYTHING?

God is usually thought to be all-powerful. But here are some things it seems he *can't* do:

God can't make another god who is even more powerful than himself.

God can't create a square circle. If it had four sides, it wouldn't be a circle; if it were a circle, it wouldn't have four sides, and so it couldn't be square.

And God couldn't make a cake too big for God to eat! If he couldn't eat something, that would mean he couldn't do everything and he wouldn't be all-powerful.

In other words, even God can't do what is literally impossible. *Perhaps he cannot be all-powerful.*

BRAIN BURN!

If God is all good, does that mean he cannot choose to do evil?

DOES GOD KNOW MY FUTURE?

If God knows *everything*, does he know what you're going to do next?

Here's a scary thought. If God does know everything, then he knows what you're going to do at 9:43 A.M. 20 years from now.

Does that mean *your future is fixed?*

Well, maybe God doesn't know the future. Maybe God knows only everything *it is possible to know*—and surely it is impossible to know the future.

Or maybe he *does* know the future. But that doesn't mean your choices won't change the future. Your future choices are all free; it's just that God can see ahead and knows what they're going to be.

If God does know the future, however, it does raise a difficult question: *why would he allow children to be born if he knew they were going to grow into evil criminals or live miserable lives?*

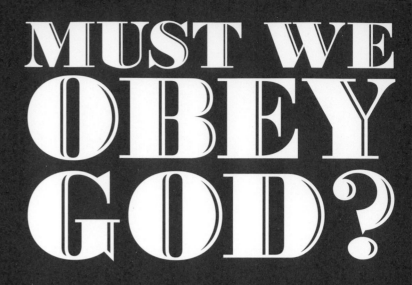

MUST WE OBEY GOD?

Most religions are very clear that God must be obeyed. Their holy books often contain stories that warn of what happens to those who don't obey. In the Bible, for example, God destroys the cities of Sodom, Gomorrah, Admah, and Zeboim, and everyone in them, because their people have not followed his laws.

But even if you think you must obey God, *how do you know what God wants?* Different people look to the same holy books and find different answers. It's hard to obey God if it's not clear what he wants!

Most religions say we should do God's will—meaning we should do what he wants us to do. But we should be careful when people tell us that they know what God wants. *How do they know?*

SHOULD WE FEAR GOD?

Some people describe themselves as "God-fearing." They think that this is a good thing. We are *supposed* to fear God. In the Bible, it says, "Fear God and keep his commandments, for this is the whole duty of man."

But *why* fear God? Well, imagine that you think that God is the most powerful thing in the whole universe. He could send you to heaven or to live forever in hell. Or he could just end your life completely. He knows everything, so when he judges you, there is nowhere for you to hide the bad things you've done. That *is* a little scary, isn't it?

But others say that because God is love, there is nothing to be afraid of. God will always do what's best for us, *because he wants what's best for us,* he knows what's best for us, and he can do anything he wants for us.

Nothing to be afraid of, then?

WHAT IF THERE IS NO

GOD?

Some people believe that there is no God. They are called *atheists*.

Would it matter if God didn't exist? Many people think it would. If the universe had no creator, and no good guy in charge, then how do we know *how* to live, *and what's the point of living in the first place?*

Most atheists disagree. They think life can be good with no God or gods. Indeed, isn't it better to treat others well just because you think you ought to, and not because you're trying to stay on God's good side? Isn't it better to appreciate life for what it is, rather than thinking too much about what might follow it?

Atheists say that living without God helps us focus on what really matters: our fellow human beings and life here on Earth.

So if God does not exist, it may not be such a disaster after all!

"Religion is something left over from the infancy of our intelligence. It will fade away as we adopt reason and science as our guidelines."

Bertrand Russell (1872–1970)
British philosopher

3

SAINTS, SINNERS, GOOD, AND EVIL

When people want to know what's right and what's wrong, they often turn to holy books or to religious leaders. And there are many rules that religions agree about. Almost all tell us to take care of the poor and not to murder or steal.

But other rules are very different. Muslims and Jews, for instance, are forbidden to eat pork, Hindus are not allowed to eat beef, and most Buddhists are vegetarian.

So, with all these different ideas floating around, *is religion the best and most reliable guide to how we should behave?*

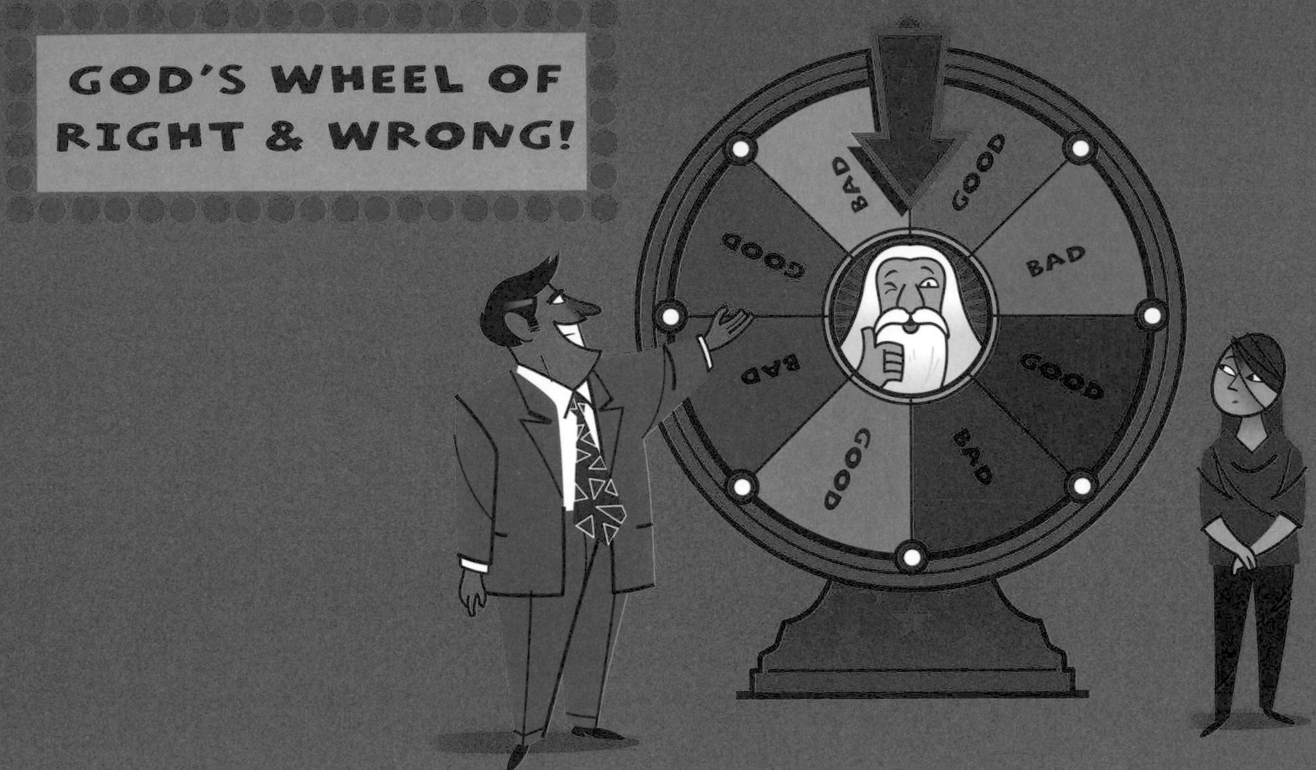

DOES RELIGION DETERMINE WHAT'S RIGHT AND WRONG?

More than 2,000 years ago, a philosopher named Plato asked, "Is what is good loved by the gods because it is good, or is it good because it is loved by the gods?"

That's a complicated question! *What did he mean?* Well, think about all the things that we think are good, like being kind and honest. Religious people believe that God wants us to be kind and honest and good in other ways, too. But *why* does God want that?

One possibility is that kindness and honesty are good things, *and God always wants what is good.*

The other possibility is that *things are good only because God wants them.* If God wanted you to be mean and dishonest, those things would be good, and their opposites, kindness and honesty, would have to be bad.

Which option do you think is true? Are things good only because God wants them, or does God want them because they are good?

If you think that things are good only because God wants them, that's a little strange. It means that everything good could be bad, and everything bad could be good.

Most people think that God wants good things because they are good. But that means *they're good anyway,* no matter what God wants. *God doesn't make them good or bad.*

So does this mean that we don't need God—or religion—to know that there is a difference between right and wrong? Or do you think that we need God to help *show us* what is good and bad?

WHAT IS A SIN?

A sin is something that a religion says is wrong. If you don't believe in God, then you don't believe in sin—but you might still believe that some things are right and some things are wrong. The difference between a sin and something that is just wrong is that *a sin breaks the law of God*.

Of course, it can be pretty scary to think you have disobeyed the most powerful thing in the universe. If you think you have sinned, you might feel very guilty and afraid of God's punishment. Some atheists think that is why religions may have created the idea of sin—it frightens people into doing what their leaders want.

What do you think? *Is sin real* or *is it an idea that religions have invented?*

AM I BORN A SINNER?

Judaism, Islam, and Christianity all tell the story of Adam and Eve, the first people God created. He allowed them to live in the Garden of Eden, which had everything they needed. *All they had to do was not eat the fruit that grew on the "tree of knowledge of good and evil."*

They blew it. Tempted by the devil, who took the shape of a snake, *they ate the fruit* and were thrown out of the garden. From that day on, some religious traditions say, every person is born guilty of the sin of Adam and Eve.

Most people don't think this story actually happened but that it teaches a lesson: *human beings are not born perfect*. Maybe a baby hasn't yet done anything wrong, but *nobody* grows up completely innocent.

For many religious people, this means we all need God's forgiveness. For others, perhaps it is simply a reminder that we are a mixture of good and bad, and we should not think that we're better than we really are.

ARE RELIGIOUS PEOPLE BETTER?

Chang is a "devout Taoist." Gurpreet is a "pious Sikh." Aisha is a "good Muslim."

Why do we describe people like this? It's because we think that being a devoted member of a religion shows that you are a good, trustworthy person. Gurpreet is "pious," meaning he follows his religion's teachings carefully. Chang is "devout," meaning that he is also dedicated to following his religion. If that is true, then you would not expect Chang to be a bad person who lies or steals (or has a bad habit of ignoring the poor and needy on his way to the temple).

Does that mean that religious people are, in general, *better* than nonreligious people? Not necessarily. When we say Aisha is a "good Muslim," we are not only saying that she is good, we are also saying something about *why* and *how* she is good. For her, the Muslim way of life gives her reasons and guidance to be good. But that does not mean other people can't be good for other reasons.

It is also possible to be a *bad* Taoist, Sikh, or Muslim, of course. Being religious does not automatically make you good.

So although having a religion to follow can help people live good lives, you can be a good, nonreligious person or a bad, religious one.

WHAT ARE SAINTS?

Many religions call people who have lived exceptionally good lives in the service of their religion "saints."

For example, the founder of Sikhism, Guru Nanak, is thought of by many as a saint. In Judaism, especially spiritual people are called *tzadik*, or "righteous ones," and they are similar to saints. The Catholic Church has many saints, such as St. Bernadette, who is said to have seen visions of Mary, the mother of Jesus, in Lourdes, France.

However, some argue that every human being is a mixture of good and bad and that it is wrong to imagine that some people are saints, meaning that they are purer than other people.

Before we decide if we might be better off without saints, we should try to understand *why* they are around. Can they be helpful role models for believers? Even if you don't believe that one person can be so much better than anyone else, you might still be able to learn something useful from the lives of saints.

"Men say I am a saint losing himself in politics. The fact is that I am a politician trying my hardest to become a saint."

Mahatma Gandhi (1869–1948)
Indian independence leader

DO RELIGIONS HELP THE POOR?

Almost every religion teaches that we have a duty to help the poor. One of the five Pillars of Islam—the things you must do to be a good Muslim—is to pay *zakaah*, a gift of money for the poor and needy. Jesus also taught, "The person who has two coats must share with the one who doesn't have any, and the person who has food must do the same."

Today and throughout history, religious groups have spent a great deal of money building temples, churches, and other places of worship.

Do you think that money would have been better spent going directly to the poor and needy? Or do you think that these temples and churches have helped poor people in some way?

Most religions put money and effort into helping the poor, but you don't need to be religious to give to charity. Anyone can try to be a compassionate and good person, whatever their beliefs.

WHAT DO RELIGIONS SAY ABOUT ANIMALS?

In some religions, such as Christianity, Judaism, and Islam, animals are put on Earth by God for our benefit. We should take care of them and not treat them cruelly, but, many argue, *they do not have souls as we do*. Animals do not go to heaven or hell.

Some of these religions have rules about which animals we are allowed to eat, but this is because some meat is said to be "unclean," not because particular animals should be respected.

In religions such as Buddhism, Hinduism, and Jainism, however, there is not a big difference between humans and animals. Followers believe that souls can live in different bodies in different lives. *The soul of a cat in this life may be the soul of a person in the future.*

In the Hindu holy book the Mahabharata, it says, "He who desires to increase his own flesh by eating the flesh of other creatures lives in misery in whatever species he may take his birth."

DO RELIGIONS TREAT MEN AND WOMEN THE SAME?

In most religions, men are given more power than women. In the Roman Catholic Church, for example, *only men* can be priests, bishops, or the Pope, the head of the church. In Islam, *only men* can be full imams, able to lead the whole mosque in prayer. In Buddhism, almost every *tulku* or lama—leaders who are said to have lived past lives—are *men*.

These religions say that although men and women are treated differently, they are still equal. Men are not better than women, but they are better suited to some roles in the religion.

However, critics say that men and women are *not* treated equally because men have more powerful positions.

In recent years, many people inside and outside religion have challenged the different treatment of men and women. In the Anglican (or Episcopalian) tradition of Christianity, for example, women can now be priests, and there are plans to allow them to be bishops, too. Some of the biggest arguments in religion today are about the role of women.

In many cultures, women are expected to cover up their bodies more than men. It's thought to be wrong for women to appear attractive to men other than their husbands.

The Koran, the holy book of Islam, says that women should dress "modestly," but Muslims disagree about how to interpret this. Some think this means not wearing short skirts or skimpy tops, but some believe that a woman should wear a headscarf to cover her hair in public. Others believe that she must also wear a *niqab* (face veil) or burqa, a loose robe that covers her whole body, including her head.

For devout Muslims, this is a question of how to understand the teachings of the Koran. But for others, it is an example of how women are not treated the same as men. *Why should women be obliged to follow stricter rules for dressing than men?*

And is it entirely up to Muslims to decide how Muslim women dress? Is it solely a matter for Catholics to decide whether a woman could be the Pope? *What do you think?*

DOES RELIGION

One of the biggest criticisms of religion is that it causes wars. Throughout history, there have been many conflicts between religions or different groups of the same religion.

For example, between the 1000s and 1200s, the Crusades saw Christian knights from European armies do battle against Muslims in the Holy Land, an area now occupied by Lebanon, Syria, Palestine, Israel, and Egypt. In Ireland in the 20th century, there were many conflicts between Protestant and Catholic Christians.

And more than 20 million people died in China between 1850 and 1864, when Hong Xiuquan and his army attempted to replace Taoism, Confucianism, and Buddhism with his own form of Christianity.

CAUSE WAR?

But are these wars *only* about religion? *Perhaps they are more about power, money, and occupying land.* Are the wars actually *political* rather than *religious?*

And some of the biggest wars in history have not been about religion at all. World War I (1914–1918) was fought mainly between Christian countries and was not about religion. World War II (1939–1945) was more of a fight between political views—communism, fascism, and democracy—than it was about religion.

It is true that religion *can* cause war, when tensions between different religious groups become too much. But it does not seem that religion is the *main cause* of war. Most wars have *political causes.* They are about who has power and who controls land, *not* who has the right religion.

IS THERE A HEAVEN?

We've seen that religious people believe different things. But almost every single one has some idea of "heaven." The idea is that, after this life, there is another life in *a different, better place*—for good people, at least.

Some of these ideas can get very complicated. In Hinduism, for example, there isn't just one heaven. Rather, there are *several different heavenly levels*.

You could argue that heaven is more important than Earth. On Earth, people live for an average of about 70 years. But many religions tell us we can live *forever* in heaven.

In fact, heaven sounds like a good idea in many ways. We get to live forever (so dying is not so scary) in a really nice place! *Is that why some people believe in heaven?*

But does heaven really exist? It doesn't seem fair to grant some people eternal life and not others, when different people are given very different opportunities in life to prove that they are worthy and good.

More important, perhaps, is that we seem to be animals of some kind. Remember, we are related to chimpanzees! But if we are animals, *how could we live forever after our bodies have died?*

IS THERE A HELL?

If there is a heaven, does that mean there is also a "hell"? Again, most religions have said that not only do the good go to heaven, but the wicked go to hell, where they are punished for *all eternity*. Inside some churches, you'll see a painting of the Last Judgment, which shows the good entering heaven and the bad being condemned to hell.

Many find the idea of hell harder to believe than heaven. If God is good, *why would he punish anyone for all eternity?* Surely no one is so bad that they deserve such punishment?

WHAT IS THE DEVIL?

If you think of hell, you'll probably think of the man in charge: the devil, or Satan. In Christianity, Judaism, and Islam, Satan was originally an *angel*, but he disobeyed God and was cast out of heaven. He's been tempting people to be evil ever since.

In other religions, there is no person or fallen angel such as the devil. Instead, there are *two opposing forces*—good and evil.

So does the devil really exist? Although some people think he does, most religious people now think of Satan as an *image* of evil rather than a real person.

The devil represents the temptation to do evil and to refuse God's will. He is not a real creature with horns and a forked tail!

WHY WOULD GOD ALLOW EVIL?

Here's a puzzle: if God is all-powerful, all-knowing, and all-good, *why is there so much evil and suffering in the world*? Why are there nasty diseases, and why do earthquakes and other natural disasters destroy lives? Why are people allowed to do horrible things to one another all the time?

It seems that God either *doesn't want* to stop these things from happening (so he's not all-good) or he *can't* stop them (so he's not all-powerful). Whichever way you look at it, it would mean that *God is not what we think he is—or perhaps he doesn't exist at all.*

Some people think they have an answer to this. They say that there are very important reasons why God must allow these things to happen. Somehow, in some way, it is better for human beings that terrible things happen. Perhaps we need bad things to give us the opportunity to do good in response. Maybe we need to learn the difference between right and wrong, and that means we have to see some very wrong things for ourselves.

Is that a good enough answer? People disagree. But most agree that *the existence of terrible things in the world is not easy to explain if a good God is in charge*.

BRAIN BURN!

If God asked you to do something you thought was wrong, would it be right to obey him?

IS GOD EVER WRONG?

Maybe bad things happen because God makes mistakes. *Is that possible?*

In ancient Greece, the gods were often shown to be like humans—they could be childish, grumpy, envious, mean, spiteful, and mischievous—and they would sometimes get things wrong.

But most of the time, God is thought to be perfect. And if he's perfect, he can't possibly make any mistakes.

So if God *is* ever wrong, *he's not God as we know him!*

COULD GOD BE WICKED?

Here's a worrying possibility: could it be that the reason why there is so much evil in the world is because God *isn't* good after all? *Could the universe be ruled by a wicked God?*

Since we don't really know for sure what God is like, or even if he exists, this is a possibility. But it doesn't look very likely. As well as suffering and pain, there are so many *good* things in the world, so much happiness, joy, and love. A wicked God would surely not allow so many wonderful things to exist in his creation!

So even if there is no good God, it seems even *less likely* that there's a wicked one.

4

LIVING WITH FAITH, GOD, SOULS, AND ANGELS

Some people don't take their religion very seriously. If you ask them what their religion is, they might say "Christian" or "Hindu," but most of the time they wouldn't even think about it.

However, for people who *do* take religion seriously, it can affect *every area of their lives*. Living a religious life can be very different from living a nonreligious one.

For some people, their religion is *so important* that they give up ordinary life and dedicate all their time to prayer and serving God in small groups. Women who do this are called nuns, and they live together in buildings called convents. Men who do the same are called monks, and they live in monasteries. They wear the same simple clothes as one another and do not own anything. They do not get married or have children.

It's time to look at some of the things that really matter in the lives of truly religious people, to see what difference it makes to have *faith*.

WHAT IS FAITH?

There's a famous story about *faith* that is told by Jews, Christians, and Muslims. Abraham, an important prophet in all three religions, wanted a child for years, but he and his wife, Sarah, could not have one. Then God made sure she got pregnant, and she had a son, Isaac.

A few years later, an angel appeared to Abraham and told him that God wanted him to *sacrifice* Isaac—*to kill him as a gift to God*. Although Isaac was the most important thing in the world to Abraham, and although he would never usually kill a person, he decided to follow God's command. But at the last minute, an angel stopped him, saying that Abraham had done enough to prove his faith in God. Isaac was saved.

The story shows that Abraham had tremendous faith in God. Faith is more than just belief—*it is a kind of trusting in God that does not ask for any explanation*. Abraham did not question—he just accepted, even though what he was asked to do appeared to be terrible. Many religious people think this is what we should all do—trust in our religious beliefs, and our God or gods, without asking for an explanation.

Some people think, however, that faith is a *bad thing*. They think that we should always rely on *reason and explanation* before we believe something, and we should not just do whatever religion asks us to do, especially if it seems wrong. With this view, Abraham was *not* a hero; he was a fool. He should never have agreed to kill his only son.

So is faith a good thing or a bad thing? People disagree, and you have to decide for yourself.

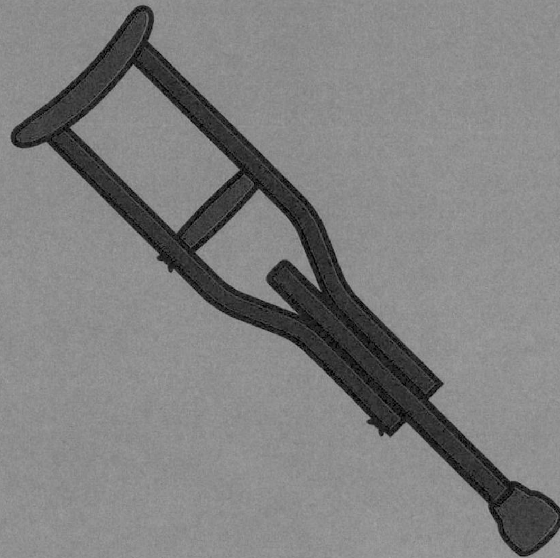

CAN FAITH HEAL PEOPLE?

Some people claim that *faith alone can heal*. If they pray and trust God, people can be healed of all sorts of illnesses.

Although there are many stories of people being miraculously cured in this way, there is no *definite proof* that any of them are *true*. People often get better for reasons we don't understand, so it is impossible to say if faith ever plays a part in healing.

So if you believe in faith healing, you do so as a matter of *faith*, not proof!

WHY DO PEOPLE WORSHIP?

Many religions include regular rituals of worship in which people praise and thank God. But *why* do they do this? And why would God want people to tell him how great he is?

One reason might be that it is important that we remain humble, meaning that we do not get too big for our britches. And praising God could help us think about *why* he is great and how we can become better people ourselves.

Another reason is that worship could be a way of reminding ourselves that we depend on God and should make him the center of our lives.

Some worship, however, is harder to explain. In some parts of the world, people sacrifice animals to God, killing them as a gift. And sometimes, during the Hindu festival of Thaipusam, worshipers pierce their faces and bodies with skewers or hooks as a sign of their devotion!

Unless you share these beliefs, it can be hard to imagine why any god would want his followers to carry out such extreme forms of worship.

"Prayer does not change God, but it does change the one who prays."

Søren Kierkegaard (1813–1855)
Danish philosopher

HOW CAN WE TALK TO GOD?

Almost everyone agrees that God does not talk *directly* to people—at least not like someone talks to you on the telephone. *So how does he tell people what he wants?*

Most religions believe that in the past, God sent prophets—human beings who were given some special knowledge of God's desires to pass on to others. Religions also have their holy books, which many believe contain God's words.

But what about *now?* Is there anyone on Earth who speaks for God today?

Almost every religion has *leaders*, but hardly any of these people claim to have a *direct* communication with God. And there is certainly not a person alive who everyone would agree can speak on God's behalf.

So although there are people who try to understand and teach what they *think* God wants, no one can claim to speak for God.

WHAT IS AN ANGEL?

Many religions have stories about messengers from God being sent to Earth. These are often "angels." Angels are like people, but they live in heaven, not on Earth. They not only bring messages, they sometimes help people, too.

But are angels real and did any of these appearances actually happen? As usual, people disagree. And even religious people disagree among themselves.

Although some people with faith believe in angels, others think they are just stories. So you don't have to believe in angels to be religious.

(And you don't need religion to believe in angels. But you might need some evidence!)

CAN THE VIRGIN MARY REALLY APPEAR IN A GRILLED CHEESE SANDWICH?

Angels aren't the only kinds of visitors from heaven. There are reports of other important religious figures appearing to people. For example, according to the Roman Catholic Church, the Virgin Mary, the mother of Jesus, has visited people in many places all over the world.

And in Sri Lanka, some Muslims believe that a satellite image of the 2004 tsunami, which killed hundreds of thousands of people, spells out the name of God, Allah. They think this means that God was punishing people for not being good enough Muslims.

Strangely, other people have reported seeing images of holy people or writings on walls and fences, cinnamon buns and chapatis, the branches of trees, frying pans, and even on the fleece of a lamb! And in 2004, an American woman sold a ten-year-old grilled cheese sandwich for $28,000, because she and others believed it showed the image of the Virgin Mary.

To nonbelievers—and many believers, too—all this is hard to accept. You can see all sorts of images and words in random shapes if you want to. Just spend half an hour looking at the clouds. How many things can you see in them? Does that mean *God* put them there?

CAN A TOOTH REALLY BE HOLY?

People often worship or pray at special places, such as temples, churches, and mosques. These are *holy places*, meaning that they have a special connection with God or the spiritual world, and so they need to be treated with extra respect.

In some religions, *objects* said to have been touched or owned by holy people in the past are also considered to be holy. A saint's glove or book would be such an object, also called a relic. One of the holiest relics in the world is in Sri Lanka. It is a tooth said to have been Buddha's.

This idea is not always used for good purposes. In the Middle Ages, for example, people used to make a lot of money selling what they claimed to be the bones of saints, when really they were just old animal bones.

Whether or not such religious objects are genuine, many people today think that the whole idea of holy places and holy things is old-fashioned. Holiness has nothing to do with *physical objects,* they might say. You can have faith and connect with God simply by thinking about him—*wherever you are and without the need for a "prop."*

If you are religious, only you can decide if places and objects are holy and how important they are to your faith.

SHOULD CHILDREN INHERIT RELIGION?

Most people who are religious raise their children to be part of the *same religion*. It's obvious why—their religion is important to them and they want their children to benefit from it in the ways that they do. And perhaps they inherited the religion from *their own parents*.

But some people argue that it is *wrong* to raise children in a particular religion. They think that everyone should be able to decide *for themselves* what is true. If you teach children just one religion, you are *brainwashing* them. Why promote one particular religion when you think it is wrong to encourage children to have one particular view about politics?

Another view is that children should be encouraged to *think for themselves*, learning about different religious and nonreligious ways of life. However, it is fine if their parents spend more time teaching them about their own faith rather than about other beliefs.

So which view is right? *How should you be raised?* Should you *inherit* religion from your parents, or should you figure it out for yourself?

BRAIN BURN!

If a baby is baptized as a Christian but is then adopted by devout Taoist parents, what religion does that baby belong to?

CAN A BABY HAVE A RELIGION?

Here's a puzzle: in many religions, there is a ceremony to welcome a baby into a particular religion. In many branches of Christianity, that ceremony is *baptism*.

But a baby cannot even talk and has no opinions about God or religion. So in what way can it make sense to say that a baby is Christian—or Jewish or Sikh? What could it mean to say a baby belongs to a particular religion?

Does a person need to be able to think for himself or herself in order to belong to a religion?

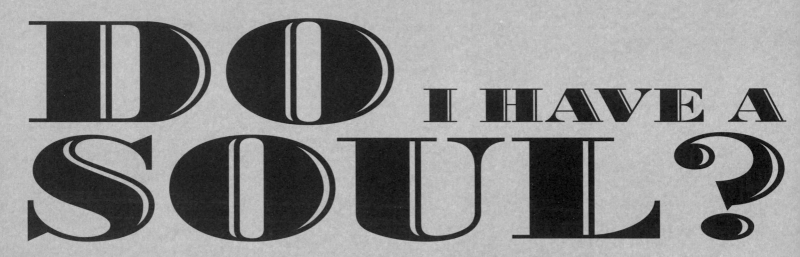

DO I HAVE A SOUL?

Who are you? *What* are you?

Take a look at yourself. What makes you *you?* You have a body and you have a brain. But what would happen if we *took away* your body and brain? *Would there be any of you left?*

Some people say the answer is *yes*. As well as your physical body and brain, you have a *soul,* which is not physical. It may live in your body for now, but when your body dies, your soul could live on, perhaps in heaven.

In many branches of Christianity, a soul cannot live separately from a body. Heaven involves the body coming back *physically,* just as Jesus was resurrected with a body. We do have a soul, but it is in some way part of our body.

In Hinduism, it is the soul that is the *real nature* of a person, rather than the body. This soul, or spirit, is called atman, and it is a Hindu's goal in life to discover his or her true self as atman and to realize oneness with Brahman, the Ultimate Reality.

Most people who are not religious do not believe in souls. They think that we are very complex animals and that when our bodies die, *we* do, too.

The question of whether we have souls turns out not only to be a very, very big one but also a very, very complicated one. Even if we *do* have souls, most people would say that it does not mean that the real you is like a *ghost* inside your body.

So if there *are* souls, what are they *made of? Where* are they? How do they separate themselves from our bodies?

CAN I PICK AND CHOOSE FROM RELIGION?

We've seen that there are many religions and many different things that people believe, even when they share the same religion. So is it possible to take just what you like from different religions, believing some things and rejecting others?

In a way, most religious people do a bit of this anyway. There is never complete agreement between members of a church, for example, even among the leaders. So people often pick and choose the parts of their religion they believe in.

But at the same time, you can't just pick the parts *you like the sound of*. The question you should ask is, *what parts are true?* And then you have to ask whether the parts you think are true *fit together*. For example, you can't believe that Jesus is the son of God and also believe that the Prophet Muhammad revealed the word of God—because Muhammad said that Jesus was *not* the son of God.

So you can decide for yourself what, if anything, you believe. But you need to have a *reason* for believing what you do. You need to think hard about what is true.

CAN I CHANGE MY RELIGION?

The religion most people have is the one they are raised with, the one they "inherit" from their family and cultural background.

But if you decide that a different religion is better, you can change. This is called conversion—because you *convert* from one religion to another.

How easy this is depends on the religion. It also depends on how important religion is to your family or community. It can be very hard to change religion if everyone around you thinks it is important that you don't.

Whatever you decide, *it is a big decision*—one you should think hard about before making.

SO WHAT SHOULD I BELIEVE?

You must know by now what the answer to this question will be! There is so much disagreement about religion that *no one can tell you what you should believe*. People may have strong opinions, but these opinions differ, so *only you* can decide who or what you think is right.

You might decide not to believe in any religion at all and be an *atheist*. Many, many people live happily and well without religion.

Other people, called *agnostics*, say that they just do not know what is true, and they live with this uncertainty. They keep an open mind and continue to ask questions, accepting that they may have no answers.

Whether you are a believer, an agnostic, or an atheist is completely up to you. Whatever you decide, you should at least now have some idea of how religion and faith pose many, many questions. Your lifetime of exploring and investigating those questions and, most important, *thinking for yourself,* has only just begun!

GLOSSARY

Words in **bold** refer to other glossary entries.

AGNOSTICISM A belief system asserting that it is not known whether **God** exists or not and that an open mind should be kept about it.

ANCIENT GREEK RELIGION The **religion** of Greece centuries before the time of **Jesus**. There were different **gods** for different things. For example, Athena was the goddess of wisdom and Poseidon was the god of the sea.

ANGEL A spiritual being who is sometimes sent by **God** to Earth as a messenger or protector.

ANIMISM A belief system asserting that all animals, plants, and objects have **souls**.

ATHEISM A belief system asserting that there is no **God** or **gods**.

BAPTISM A Christian ceremony in which a baby, child, or adult is sprinkled or covered with water and welcomed as a member of the **religion**.

BIBLE The Hebrew Bible is the **holy** book of **Judaism**. Christians call this the Old Testament, and together with the New Testament, it forms the Christian Bible. Both Bibles are collections of many shorter books.

BIG BANG The massive explosion that scientists believe brought our **universe** into existence. The big bang took place about 13 billion years ago.

BISHOP A high-ranking priest in the Christian **church**. The head of some churches is called the archbishop.

BUDDHISM A **religion** that grew largely in India and Southeast Asia. It focuses on the spiritual development of the individual rather than on the **worship** of **gods**.

CHRISTIANITY A **religion** whose members believe that **Jesus** Christ is the son of **God** and that he was sent to Earth to take away the **sins** of the world. It is the largest **religion** in the world.

CHURCH A building in which Christians meet to **worship**, or a particular group of Christians, such as the Roman Catholic Church or the United Methodist Church.

COMMUNION A Christian ceremony in which people consume bread and wine, which they believe either symbolize or become the body and blood of **Jesus**.

CONFUCIANISM An ancient Chinese philosophy that some consider to be a **religion** because it involves **rituals** and the **worship** of ancestors. Tradition, humanity, and loyalty are some of its most important values.

DEITY A god or goddess, usually assuming human or animal form.

FAITH Belief that is based on trust rather than proof or strong evidence.

GOD Usually a supernatural being who created and controls the **universe**, including life on Earth.

GODS Supernatural beings who are each responsible for different aspects of human, animal, and natural life.

HEAVEN A place where good people who have obeyed **God** are believed to live forever after death.

HELL A place of punishment where wicked people who have disobeyed **God** in their lifetime are believed to be sent after death.

HINDUISM A **religion**, the third largest in the world, originating along the Indus Valley in what is modern-day Pakistan. Hindus believe their real nature to be a **spirit** called atman, and they strive to achieve unity with Brahman, the Ultimate Reality. Hinduism has thousands of **gods**, or **deities**, who can help believers find their path to Brahman, their one true **God**.

HOLY Spiritually pure; sacred.

IMAM A leader of a **mosque** or **Muslim** community.

ISLAM A **religion** that rose in the A.D. 600s under the leadership of the **Prophet Muhammad** in what is now Saudi Arabia. It is the second-largest and fastest-growing **religion** in the world.

JAINISM One of the oldest surviving belief systems in the world, Jainism is an Indian **religion** that emphasizes respect for all life, even the smallest insects, and the need to free the **soul** from the body.

JESUS A man who lived 2,000 years ago in what is now Israel. Christians believe that Jesus, or Jesus Christ, is the son of **God** and that he was sent to Earth to take away the **sins** of the world.

JEW A person can be a Jew by being born to a Jewish mother or by joining the **religion** of **Judaism**. Many people call themselves Jews because their ancestors were Jewish, not because they follow **Judaism** as a **religion**.

JUDAISM Originating with the **prophet** Abraham in the Middle East, Judaism is the **religion** of the Jewish people, who, according to the **Bible**, were chosen by **God**.

KORAN Often written as "Qur'an," the **holy** book of **Islam** said to be the direct word of **God**, which came to the **Prophet Muhammad** through the archangel Jibril (Gabriel) between A.D. 610 and 632.

MEDITATION A spiritual practice in which people try to become aware of their true nature or the nature of **God**. Meditation is common in the **religions** of **Buddhism**, **Hinduism**, and **Sikhism**.

MOSQUE A building in which **Muslims** meet to **worship**.

MUSLIM A follower of **Islam**.

PHILOSOPHER A person who thinks carefully and seriously about questions that don't have factual answers, such as *how should we live?* and *what is knowledge?*

PLATO One of the greatest **philosophers** in history, Plato lived in ancient Greece. His ideas about the difference between mind (or **soul**) and body influenced Christian and nonreligious thought for centuries.

POLITICAL Relating to the decisions and interests of the governments and rulers of different countries or groups of people.

PRAY To talk to **God** in some way, usually by asking him for help or guidance or by **worshiping** or thanking him.

PRIEST A leader of a **church** or Christian community.

PROPHET A person to whom it is said that **God** has given special knowledge. The prophet can then pass on God's message to others.

PROPHET MUHAMMAD Muhammad is usually called the founder of **Islam**. **Muslims** believe that his task was to restore the true **religion** of **prophets** such as Adam, Noah, Abraham, Moses, and **Jesus**.

RABBI A Jewish religious teacher, often the leader of a **synagogue** or Jewish community.

REASON The human capacity to think through ideas, relying as little as possible on hunches, intuitions, or people who claim to already know the answers.

RELIGION An organized system of belief that involves some kind of acceptance of a reality beyond the physical world that we see around us.

RESURRECTED Brought back to life.

RITUAL A repeated series of actions that are often part of a religious ceremony.

ROMAN CATHOLICISM A major branch of **Christianity** that traces its roots back to the first followers of **Jesus**. Its head is the Pope, and its headquarters is Vatican City, an independent city-state in Rome, Italy.

SCIENCE An attempt to understand how the world works by experiment, measurement, and observation.

SIKHISM A **religion** founded in 15th-century India by Guru Nanak. Followers use **meditation** to attempt to achieve a spiritual union with **God**.

SIN Something that breaks the law of **God**.

SOUL The part of a person that is believed to be separate from the body and, some say, can live on after the body has died.

SPIRIT A being or power that is not physical.

SYNAGOGUE A building in which **Jews** meet to **worship**.

TAOISM A Chinese religious and philosophical system (sometimes written as "Daoism") that is concerned with living in harmony with the natural energy of the **universe**.

TEMPLE A religious building in which believers meet to **worship**. Followers of **Buddhism** and **Hinduism** **pray** in temples.

TORAH Five books containing the major texts of Jewish religious law. The first five books of both the Jewish and Christian **Bible** are: Genesis, Exodus, Leviticus, Numbers, and Deuteronomy.

UNITED NATIONS An international organization to which almost all of the world's governments belong. The United Nations tries to help countries experiencing difficulties caused by war, poverty, or natural disaster.

UNIVERSE The entire physical world, containing all the planets, all the stars, and all of space and time.

WORSHIP To praise and give thanks to **God** or **gods**.

INDEX

FURTHER READING

BOOKS

The Philosophy Files by Stephen Law
The Philosophy Files 2 by Stephen Law
Really, Really Big Questions about Life, the Universe, and Everything by Stephen Law
Really, Really Big Questions about Space and Time by Mark Brake
What Do You Believe? by Aled Jones

WEBSITES

World religions:
www.bbc.co.uk/religion/religions

Facts and figures about religions:
www.religionfacts.com

Critical-thinking fun:
www.skeptic.com/junior_skeptic

HOW TO THINK & ASK QUESTIONS

Don't just ask *what* people believe—think about *why* they believe it. Here are three useful *why* questions:

1. *Why do people want to believe some things and not others?* Think about their *motives*. Ideas are not just true or false—they can be appealing or unappealing. If we really want something to be true, then we might believe it, even if it's false.

2. *Why should we believe the things that religious and nonreligious people believe are true?* Think about the *reasons* and *evidence* for different beliefs. What *good reasons* can someone give to show that their holy book is the word of God? What *evidence* does another person have for saying that God doesn't exist?

3. *Why do people belong to a particular religion?* It's not always about belief or what is true. People might belong to a religion in order to be a member of the same group as their family or others from their country.